ROMANOVS REVISITED

1860 – 1960

David William Cripps

To Christine, with all my love for her support and help with this book

© 2005 by David W Cripps
All Rights Reserved

Published by

ROSVALL ROYAL BOOKS
Enåsen – Falekvarna
521 91 FALKÖPING, Sweden
tel: 46-515-37105 fax: 46-515-37165
e-mail: ted.rosvall@telia.com

ISBN 91-975671-1-6
Elanders Gummessons, Falköping 2005

FRONT COVER
Tsar Nicholas II with his wife Alexandra and their firstborn, Grand Duchess Olga. A happy family!

BACK COVER
A family group in 1896. From left to right: The dowager Empress Marie with baby Olga, Grand Duchess Xenia with baby daughter Irina, Grand Duchess Olga, Tsar Nicholas II and Empress Alexandra.

David William Cripps was born in London and educated in the home counties. He grew up between London and Norfolk. He has always had a passion for Victorian Royalty, especially the Romanovs. At the moment he works as a historical researcher for TV companies. The latest programme being planned is on Royalty and their gardens, which will be screened later this year.

INTRODUCTION

Most people enjoy looking through old photographs, especially when they are over one hundred years old. Even more so, of course, when the pictures show members of a once great dynasty that disappeared towards the end of the Great War, amidst revolution and bloodshed.

Some of these images are made so much more poignant because we know what happened to the Imperial children, or at least to some of them, over 80 years ago. In this book, I have tried to mix the formal with the informal and I have also included the brothers, sisters, mother and some of the cousins of the last anointed Tsar. All of the photographs come from private collections and even if some have been seen before, hopefully some are new to the reader, which is the whole point of any new book on this once illustrious family.

My own interest started when I was very young with a TV programme called "Children of Destiny" focusing on the last Imperial children and particularly Anastasia. When it was screened, I wanted to believe the version that she did survive the massacre and was truly a lost princess.

As an adult, in view of the results of the DNA testing, I now know that the woman claiming to be Anastasia could not have been her. But, how did she know so much?

When you look at some of these images it is like a diary of their lives in photographs. I have tried to include a lot of images of the Tsar's mother, brothers and sisters, since they were some of the most facinating personalities of Imperial Russia. To widen the sphere, I have also added pictures of other, lesser-known, members of the large Romanov family.

I would like to thank the following people without whom this book would never have seen the light of day: Mark Fricker, Nicholas LeCornu, Sophie Dupré, Clive Farahar, Josephine Lister and Peter Henery, with many thanks for their support, friendship and love. I would also like to thank Her Highness Princess Olga Romanoff for lending me some interesting images and for sharing some of her memories, Robin Piguet from Hatchards, Ian Shapiro of Argyll Etkin Ltd and Dr P Shelley for their historical knowledge and great assistance.

London in September 2005

David William Cripps
1 Chadwick Mews
Thames Road, Chiswick
London W4 3QX

Tsar Nicholas II surrounded by the members of his extended family. This early royal collage shows the Emperor, his wife, mother, daughters, sisters and brother as well as his uncles, aunts and cousins, in fact most of the Imperial Family of 1900.

Tsar Alexander II, the Tsar Liberator. The most liberal of all Tsars he was to die horrifically on the day that he was to sign a manifesto. His tragic death by assassination was perhaps the cruellest blow to Imperial prestige and was to set the course that led to the demise of the dynasty nearly forty years later. The reclusive Empress Marie suffered from ill health and as a result shunned society life and found it difficult to be an Empress. By the late 1860s the love that Alexander II had for her since she was a girl had practically diminished. In many ways the Tsar and she were temperamentally unsuited to each other, but they had six children and it was impossible to divorce. When she died in 1880 Alexander II married morganatically Princess Catherine Dolgorouky who was created Princess Yourievsky. They had an incredible romance by which they produced a boy and two girls before they were married, much to the horror of Empress Marie's children. Below, the future Tsar Alexander III and his wife, who was also renamed Marie. 1870.

Grand Duchess Marie (1853-1920), Tsar Alexander II's only daughter, with her younger brothers, Serge and Paul, to whom she was extremely close, as her mother was often ill. They would all travel with the Empress and it was on these journeys that Serge was to meet his future wife Ella (as a baby). At the time of this photograph in 1863 she had not even been born. Grand Duchess Marie was married to Queen Victoria's second son, Alfred, Duke of Edinburgh, in 1874.

Grand Duke Alexander and Grand Duke Vladimir. In this particular portrait Grand Duke Alexander looks extremely like his son, Nicholas II at the same age. This was taken shortly after the boy's father Tsar Alexander II had ascended the throne in 1856.

Tsarevitch Nicholas (1843-1865) shortly after his father's accession, 1856. He was the blessed child of both parents and was given the finest education to enable him to be a forward-thinking Tsar. About this time he first saw a photograph of the young Princess Dagmar. He started to collect her cartes de visite, determined that one day he would marry her. So you could say he fell in love with a photograph.

Nicholas Alexandrovitch, the Tsarevitch, at 22. He was the hope of a nation but tragically he was dying of pneumonia.

Princess Dagmar of Denmark at 16.

The Tsarevitch at Cannes, shortly before his death.

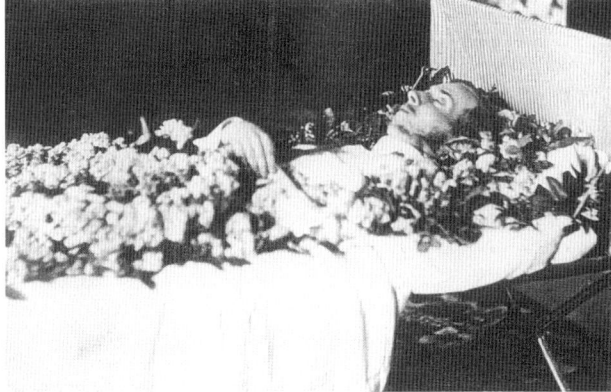

1865. A tsarevitch dies in Nice in the South of France. A panic-stricken Princess Dagmar of Denmark arrives from Copenhagen to see the man, to whom she was briefly engaged.

The Danish Princesses, whose good looks had enraptured an Emperor and captivated his son. They looked towards this Scandinavian country for suitable brides, but the British Queen was also looking for a wife for her son, the Prince of Wales, and so Alexandra (on the right) went to England and Dagmar (on the left) went to Russia. 1861

The young Princess Dagmar and her sister Thyra and brother Waldemar photographed at the time of their sister Alexandra's wedding to the Prince of Wales. 1863

Princess Dagmar of Denmark (1847-1928), who was engaged to the dying Tsarevitch. Legend has persisted to this day that Nicholas asked his brother Alexander to marry his fiancée. This they did in what was to become one of the happiest marriages, but which had started in such awful circumstances.

A fiancée in mourning 1865. Both the Princess and her parents, the King and Queen of Denmark, felt that the Russian throne had slipped through Dagmar's fingers.

The new Tsarevitch. After the premature death of his brother, the future Tsar Alexander III took on a role that was not easy. He had not had the education nor the training that had been given to his brother so readily, but in time he was to become a strong Tsar with the capacity to understand his own limitations. He ruled the empire and his family in the same way and as such, he kept the Imperial household under control.

1866. Tsar, Alexander II (1818-1881), Empress Marie (1824-1880) and the engaged couple, the future Tsar Alexander III and his bride, Dagmar, Princess of Denmark. This type of carte de visite was called a composite photograph, taken from different groups and put together. They were extremely popular with the Victorians.

A collage of Alexander II with his wife Empress Marie, his son Tsarevitch Alexander with his wife Dagmar, his daughter Marie and son Grand Duke Vladimir with his wife Marie Pavlovna. Completing the group are the Emperor's younger sons, Alexis, Serge and Paul and his grandsons, the future Nicholas II and Grand Duke George. This example of an early cabinet photograph dates from 1871 and became popular with the masses as it clearly depicted the Tsar and his immediate family.

An unusual portrait of the future Alexander III with Dagmar, who was already pregnant with her first child. 1867

The first born. The future Tsar Nicholas II has a piggyback-ride with his mother, who had been renamed Marie. She was following the trend of the time, as her sister Alexandra had been photographed with the future George V in a similar pose, to show how healthy she was. Copenhagen, Summer 1869.

A formal portrait of Marie Feodorovna and her son Tsar Nicholas II in 1870. At this time he was third in line to the throne and his mother's principal interest was to arrange, in the Great Hall, a playroom for her son. At one end was erected a complete gymnasium along the side, two wooden American mountains, ranged with polished runways down which all of the children, in time, rushed on wheeled trollies. There were toy railways, swings, rocking horses and a merry-go-round. It was paradise for young children.

HIH Grand Duchess Alexandra Josephovna (1830–1911). She married the second son of Tsar Nicholas I, Grand Duke Konstantin Nikolaievitch. Her two daughters were Queen Olga of Greece and Duchess Vera of Württemberg. Her eldest son had been banished and was later murdered by the Bolsheviks, as was her third son Grand Duke Dimitri and four of her grandsons. She herself managed to obtain the ripe old age of 81 and died six years before the revolution.

Grand Duke Konstantin Nikolaievitch (1827-1892) and Grand Duke Nikolai Konstantinovitch (1850-1918) in 1856. In 1874, the boy was to get involved in a scandal that was to grieve Alexander II so that he banisheded him from Court. He was sent to Tashkent and never returned. During the revolution of 1917 he sent a telegram to congratulate the provisional government and Kerenskij its leader, but during the Bolshevik horror he was murdered in early 1918. The one thing he had forgotten was that he was still

Grand Duke Mikhail Nikolaievitch (1832–1909) was the fourth son of Tsar Nicholas I. In 1862 Alexander II appointed him Viceroy of the Caucasus. He was to become the longest-lived grand duke of his generation.

Grand Duke Alexei (1850-1908) on his tour of America in the year 1871. He was photographed by M R Brady, who was a famous civil war photographer. A member of the Imperial Family thought that gallivanting across America was a dreadful mistake, but Alexei received a tremendous reception in New York, and in Washington he met President Grant. Following his return to Russia he was appointed a Grand Admiral of the Navy. He did not distinguish himself in this post, being opposed to any naval reform. The Grand Duke held this position from 1888 until his death in 1908.

Grand Duke Nikolai Nikolaievitch the elder (1831–1891) was the third son of Nicholas I, but is more famous for being the father of Grand Duke Nikolai Nikolaievitch, Commander of the Russian Army in World War I before Tsar Nicholas II became Supreme Commander, to the absolute horror of most of the family.

1870. The young Marie Feodorovna, who was considered such a huge success by the St Petersburg society.

A powerful group. A future Tsar, his future Empress and her sister, a future Queen of England. The three had such fun together especially when Alexander III was invested by the Prince of Wales with the Order of the Garter at the Anitchkof Palace. In accordance with tradition, the star, the ribbon, the collar, the sword and the actual garter were carried on long narrow velvet cushions. As the Prince and his entourage entered the Throne Room, a perfectly audible feminine voice cried out in English "Oh my dear, do look at them, they look exactly like a row of wet nurses carrying babies". The two sisters exploded with laughter and Alexander III fought manfully for a while to keep a straight face until he caught sight of a member of the Prince of Wales' staff, carrying his cushion in a peculiarly maternal fashion that it so excited the risibility of the Royal sisters. Alexander also succumbed, his colossal frame quivered with mirth. Never since the institution of the order in 1348, has the Garter been conferred amidst such hilarity. Hopefully Queen Victoria was not informed.

*The first daughter, Xenia, 1876.
The future Tsar Alexander III had so wanted a
daughter so she was a great addition to the family.*

*Twins in everything but age. Marie on the right, Alexandra on the left.
Not only were they sisters, they were best friends and they liked to
dress identically. The year is 1873.*

*The eldest son, the future Tsar Nicholas II,
photographed wearing a sailor suit which was
fashionable at the time, 1873.*

A glorious image of the future Tsar Nicholas II, his sister Xenia and brother George in 1877.

Marie Feodorovna with her three eldest children Nicholas, George and Xenia. At this time she was quite young and had plenty of time to devote to her three eldest children. George was the joker and years later when Nicholas was Tsar and after George's death he would lock himself away in his study and people would hear him laughing at the jokes that George had written to him.

1881. The death of the Tsar Liberator was a blow that nobody expected, except for Tsar Alexander II himself.

Tsar Alexander III (1845-1894), whose nephews and nieces nicknamed him "Uncle Fatty".

A proud mother, Marie Feodorovna, photographed in the year 1877.

The new Tsar, Alexander III, was never to be as liberal as his father.

*The new Tsar, Alexander III's beloved consort, Empress Marie.
He called her "the Angel of Russia". This was a true nickname, because
she managed to charm both the entire Romanov clan and the ministers,
and helped him to rule capably. For his entire adult life she
was everything. When he died she was absolutely desolate.*

Empress Marie with her children Xenia, Michael and George and members of her household in 1890 at the Finnish Fishing Lodge called Langinkoski. The lodge was small and extremely simple. The Tsar liked to chop his own firewood and the Tsarina cooked for her children. She also went as far as forbidding the Tsar to smoke indoors and insisted he go outside on the full-length veranda, as she claimed this little place was far too small to have smoke wafting all over it. After the Tsar's death Empress Marie never visited the lodge again.

The young Tsarevitch Nicholas, in uniform.

The Tsarevitch Nicholas with his mother in 1888. This was the year of the famous train crash at Borki, in which all of Tsar Alexander III's family were aboard. Grand Duchess Vladimir, hoping that the entire family would be wiped out, thus enabling her husband to become Tsar, is reputed to have said: "We shall never have such a chance again". Right: A picture, taken at the same time, with the other children, Michael, Xenia, Olga and George.

Empress Marie and her eldest daughter, Grand Duchess Xenia. She was sweet natured, and inherited much of her mother's great charm, but not her looks.

Nicholas II's childhood friend was Grand Duke Alexander Mikhailovitch (1866-1933). They met as boys became brothers-in-law as men and remained friends until the end. Alexander fell in love with Alexander's III elder daughter Xenia, but it was Empress Marie, her mother, who would not agree to an early marriage, as Xenia was 17 when it was first discussed. Finally the Grand Duke's father confronted the Empress and she eventually gave in and allowed their marriage.

Grand Duchess Xenia Alexandrovna (1875-1960) at the age of 18.

Ella and her sister Alix with the rest of the Hesse children were very close to the British Royal Family due to the loss of their mother. Standing left to right: Prince Albert Victor of Wales, Princess Helena, Prince Ernest of Hesse, The Prince of Wales, Princess Ella of Hesse, Prince Christian of Schleswig-Holstein, Prince George of Wales, Prince Christian Victor of Schleswig-Holstein, Princess Victoria of Wales, Grand Duke Louis of Hesse-Darmstadt. Seated: Princess Alix of Hesse, the Princess of Wales, Princess Victoria of Hesse, Princess Louise of Wales. On the ground: Princess Maud of Wales, Prince Albert of Schleswig-Holstein and Princess Irene of Hesse. 1882.

A family group in mourning for their mother 1880. Princess Ella of Hesse, who was to marry into the Russian Imperial House in June 1884, is here photographed with her brother and sisters, left to right: Ernie, Victoria, Irene and Alix, the future Empress of Russia.

A stunning portrait of a young Ella.

The Saint, Ella (1864-1918), Princess of Hesse and by Rhine, and Grand Duchess of Russia. A ravishing beauty with a rare intelligence, a delightful sense of humour, infinite patience, hospitality of thought, a generous heart, all gifts were hers, so wrote Grand Duke Alexander. Photographed 1884.

The Sinner, Serge (1857–1905). "Obstinate, arrogant, disagreeable, he flaunted his many peculiarities in the face of an entire nation", claimed Grand Duke Alexander, "his only redeeming feature being that he married Ella". The Grand Duke Alexander also claimed that she was too proud to complain. In Ella's many notes and letters she says completely the opposite and would insist to her grandmother, Queen Victoria, how supremely happy she was. The Queen made a wry note that "why is it Ella keeps insisting she is so happy?" The old Queen was no fool, having dealt with a variety of personalities over 50 years.

Nicholas, the Tsarevitch, at the age of 21. He was absolutely besotted with a golden-haired princess, who lived so far away. He also had feelings for a ballerina, who was near at hand.

Mathilde Kshesinskaya (1872-1971), who lived to be almost 100 years old. Her first love was the Tsarevitch Nicholas and their affair was to last for about two years. After the revolution she went on to marry Grand Duke Andrew. They had enjoyed a secret relationship since 1902 and had a son called Vladimir "Vova" (1902-1974).

A Grand Duke, a Greek Princess and then tragedy.

Left: Grand Duke Paul (1860-1919), who was the most gentle of Tsar Alexander II's sons, photographed in 1894.

Middle: The engagement of Grand Duke Paul and Princess Alexandra of Greece, daughter of his first cousin, Queen Olga of Greece.

Right: The young Grand Duchess Alexandra (1870-1891) in court dress, shortly after her marriage on June 17th 1889.

Grand Duchess Marie Pavlovna was born in 1890. Seventeen months later Grand Duchess Alexandra died at the age of 21, shortly after the birth of Grand Duke Dimitri Pavlovitch. The grieving husband turned away from his children in the wake of this catastrophe. Several years later Paul was to marry again.

Motherless children: Dimitri Pavlovitch and Marie Pavlovna were almost like twins and were inseparable. Throughout her life, Dimitri was Marie's strongest attachment.

A family of hope. Paul with his two children, Dimitri and Marie, his sister-in-law Ella and brother Serge in 1892. They are still in mourning for Paul's first wife. Eventually he went travelling. He had always been fragile and with the death of his wife he removed himself from his children. By 1902 he had to all intents and purposes gone to live in Paris, taking three million Roubles of his own money with him. He had decided to marry his mistress, a divorcee called Olga Pistolkors, who had him completely under her control. The Tsar and family were horrified at Paul's elopement. In many ways he sacrificed everything, including his children, for a woman that members of the Imperial Family considered not worthy of it. By 1910 the Tsar relented, allowing his uncle and new wife to return to Russia.

Grand Duke Serge with his wards, Grand Duchess Marie and Grand Duke Dimitri. Grand Duchess Marie in her memoirs considered his sweetness towards them to be almost feminine. In 1905, a sort of dress rehearsal year for the 1917 revolution, the Grand Duke was murdered.

Ella. After the assassination of her husband she took up a new vocation. She had always been extremely religious, now she made it her life's work to help the poor of Moscow. She opened a convent and founded a community. In the revolution of 1917 Kaiser Wilhelm did his utmost to save her, as when she had been young he had desperately wanted to marry her. In April 1918 she was sent to Perm with five of her relatives. She was imprisoned in a deserted school building and in the dead of night with the rest of the family and Sister Barbara who had accompanied her, they were thrown down a mineshaft. Despite the loyalty of untold thousands of Russian people and although she had given up a life of grandeur and position, the Bolsheviks murdered her because of her royal birth.

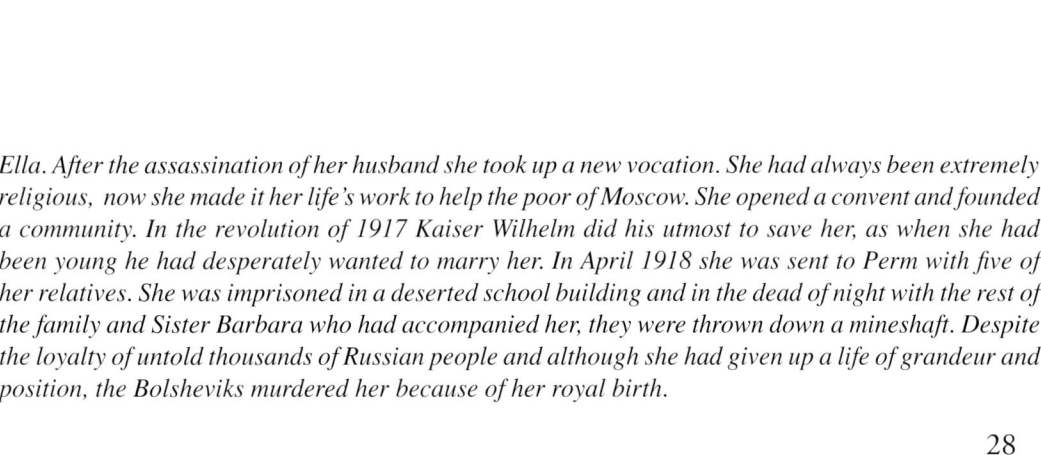

Family group taken in the Crimea at the time of the engagement of Xenia to her cousin Alexander Mikhailovitch. From left to right: Tsarevitch Nicholas, behind him his brother, George, his grandfather, King Christian of Denmark, Empress Marie, Queen Louise of Denmark, the Princess of Wales. In front: The newly engaged couple, Alexander and Xenia with her cousin, Princess Maud of Wales in the middle, her father Tsar Alexander III behind, Princess Victoria of Wales behind him, Grand Duke Michael and Grand Duchess Olga in front.

Tsar Alexander III in his hunting outfit in Poland in the spring of 1893. He lacked the great human capacity to make friends. One man whom he did trust was Pobiedontzff, the protagonist of autocracy.

Last holiday at Livadia before the Tsar's illness. The Imperial family of 1893. From left to right: Tsarevitch Nicholas, Grand Duke George, Empress Marie, Grand Duchesses Olga and Xenia, Grand Duke Michael, Tsar Alexander III.

The last informal portrait of Tsar Alexander III in August 1893.

Grand Duke Michael comes of age. The twenty one year old Grand Duke was the favourite child of Alexander III and with the death of his brother Grand Duke George became heir apparent to the Russian throne, but not the Tsarevitch, as Empress Alexandra prevented it.

1896. The Tsar's sister Olga (1882-1960) does high kicks for the camera. At the time of her father's death she was only 12 and because of this and her natural mischievousness she became very close to Nicholas and Alexandra, loving them deeply. In her memoirs it is the Dowager Empress, her mother, who comes in for the most critical comment, as she and Olga had many fights.

An intimate view of a family. Nicholas II, photographed with his mother and his sister Xenia at the Kaiser Villa in Denmark, where they often went to have tea. The Kaiser Villa still stands to this day.

The mother of the future Empress, Princess Alice (1843-1878), Grand Duchess of Hesse. She was to die at the early age of 35. A portrait like this one was always kept by the last Empress of Russia in her mauve boudoir.

Days with Grandmama. Queen Victoria surrounded by members of her family in the summer of 1891. From left to right: Princess Alix of Hesse, an Indian servant, Prince Henry of Battenberg, Princess Victoria of Hesse. Seated: Princess Beatrice, Queen Victoria, The Grand Duke of Hesse, who was to die the following year, and the Battenberg children, including Ena, future Queen of Spain. At this time the Queen was trying to persuade her favourite granddaughter to marry Eddy, the Duke of Clarence, and one day become Queen of England. However, Alix would not budge and amazingly Queen Victoria surrendered.

Alix photographed at the age of 16, although it was to be the following year that her feelings deepened for Nicholas. She had first met him at the age of 12 at Ella's wedding. Years later when she was Empress she admitted to Nicholas in a private letter how her childish heart already went out to him in deep love.

Empress Marie, 1894. The anxiety for her husband's health brought on acute lumbago. Shortly before the Tsar's death the Empress Marie could hardly move.

Tsar Alexander III is dying. He was suffering from Bright's disease, a kidney disorder for which there was no cure even though he had the best physicians. He was advised by them to go to Corfu but he would not hear of it and said: "a Russian Tsar must die in Russia". So he went to Livadia. By October the Tsar's health declined rapidly and his son's fiancée, Princess Alix of Hesse, was sent for. He insisted on getting up to greet the future Russian Empress. On November 1st he passed away.

Princess Alix of Hesse in 1894. The Empress particularly disliked the Princess's reserve, but in the end Tsar Alexander III gave his consent to the betrothal and she had no choice other than to give in graciously.

A glamorous portrait of the young couple at the time of their engagement. Little did they realise that the few days they were to spend at Walton-on-Thames and then at Windsor to be with the Princess' grandmother, the Queen, before they were married in the winter of 1894, was to be the only honeymoon period they were to have. By the end of the year they were Tsar and Empress. Had the Tsarevitch's father not been so ill, Queen Victoria would have kept Princess Alix with her until the spring wedding, which was planned for the following year.

The new Tsar Nicholas II at the age of 26. He was extremely frightened by his new position, as for some reason his parents had tried to keep him in a perpetual state of adolescence. A precarious situation, as he was now ruler of one sixth of the earth. He turned to his mother for help but her counsel was not always wise, though well-meaning. She had been his father's helpmate, but his father had made all the decisions. This was perhaps the biggest mistake that Alexander III had ever made in the upbringing of his eldest son.

At the beginning of Nicholas and Alexandra's married life they lived with the Dowager Empress, which was a huge mistake. The young couple needed their own residence but the dowager thwarted the situation. Charming and amiable, with good intentions, she was overbearing and wished to take precedence. A few months later the young Tsar and his wife moved to their own residence. Alexandra, however, never forgot the treatment she received in the home of her mother-in-law.

Grand Duchess Elisabeth (Ella) who was seven and a half years older than her sister Alix. Queen Victoria was of the opinion that Ella was determined that Alix should marry the Tsarevitch and she was therefore not pleased when Alix went to stay with her sister in 1889. Alix was 17 and Nicholas was 21 – "a dangerous age when young men and pretty girls fall in love".

Alexandra in 1896. The grandeur of her new position made the young Empress isolated and lonely, with only her husband and sister for advice and protection. Unfortunately she felt that there was no one else that she could trust.

Ella, Grand Duchess of Russia, who had done so much to encourage the match between her sister and Nicholas, who was her nephew by marriage. She wrote in a private note how glad she was to go down on her knees in respect of her sister's new exalted position.

Tsarskoe Selo Palace with the young Tsar Nicholas II and Empress Alexndra on the occasion of the visit of Prince Adolf of Schaumbourg-Lippe. From left to right: Grand Duke Paul Alexandrovitch, Prince Adolf, Empress Alexandra of Russia, Grand Duke Serge Mikhailovitch, Nicholas II, Prince Georg Romanovsky, Grand Duchess Marie Pavlovna the elder, The Duchess of Leuchtenberg, (Anastasia, née a Princess of Montenegro), Princess Eugenia Romanovsky/Oldenburg, Grand Duke Serge Alexandrovitch and Grand Duke Vladimir Alexandrovitch. The young Empress was terrified by these family occasions, though at this time she received a lot of goodwill from the Imperial family. Sadly this was not to last.

1896. Tsar Nicholas II.
Nicholas and Alexandra were to be the youngest sovereigns of Europe.

1896. Empress Alexandra, spectacularly beautiful and flamboyantly dressed, looked every inch what an Empress should be.

After the Coronation festivities a family group was taken at Ella and Serge's country house, Ilinskoie, near Moscow. From left to right, the young Tsar, in front his young Empress, the rest standing: Princess Victoria of Battenberg (Empress Alexandra's sister), Grand Duke Paul, Grand Duke Ernest of Hesse, Crown Prince Ferdinand of Romania, Crown Princess Marie of Romania, Princess Beatrice of Edinburgh and Saxe-Coburg. Next to the young Empress, seated from left to right: Grand Duchess Ella, Grand Duke Serge, The Duchess of Edinburgh and of Saxe-Coburg and Gotha and Grand Duchess Victoria Melita of Hesse. This photograph disguises a very unhappy family group, as during the coronation festivities a fete had been arranged in the open air for the people of Moscow and the peasantry of the surrounding villages. The measures taken by the police were inadequate and a huge number of men, women and children were trampled to death. The Tsar and his Empress appeared on the balcony of the pavilion of the Khodinka field with the rest of the Imperial Family, not knowing that under the pavilion many of their loyal subjects lay dead. Grand Duke Serge who was the Governor General of Moscow was directly responsible but Nicholas was too young to stand up to his uncle. Many considered it inappropriate that on the night of this disaster, the Imperial couple held a ball, but they did not realise that they had been forced into it by the brothers of Alexander III and that most of the Imperial Family had spent days in the hospital visiting the surviving victims. It was however considered a bad omen for the start of a reign.

September 1896. The Tsar with his wife's uncle, Arthur, Duke of Connaught (1850-1942), who had represented Queen Victoria at the Coronation of his niece and nephew-in-law in May of that year. This had much mortified the Duke and Duchess of York (later George V and Queen Mary) who deeply resented it that the Connaughts had been sent instead of them. Considering how long Queen Mary was to live, and the fact that she so enjoyed history and pageantry, this was rather short sighted on the part of the old Queen.

Grand Duchess Vladimir and Grand Duchess Anastasia Mikhailovna (1860–1922) with their pages at the May Coronation of Nicholas and Alexandra. Queen Victoria thought that May Coronations were unlucky.

On the day in September 1896 that Queen Victoria became the longest reigning monarch in British history, her granddaughter Alexandra came to stay with her at Balmoral. From left to right: the Gillie, the Duke of Connaught, Princess Patricia of Connaught, Tsar Nicholas II, Queen Victoria, Princess Helena Victoria, Empress Alexandra, the Duchess of Connaught, Princess Margaret of Connaught.

An Empress and her first baby. Alexandra was so devoted to her baby daughter that officials thought she had no interest apart from being in the Imperial nursery. Even Queen Victoria commented: "Alicky is totally wrapped up in her splendid baby". 1896.

Grand Duchess Olga in 1898. A delightful photograph of the little Grand Duchess and her doll.

Grand Duchess Tatiana in 1898. The Tsar himself commented that she was a beautiful child.

The Grand Duchesses Olga and Tatiana with their first cousin, Princess Elizabeth of Hesse, in 1901. The little Princess was to die less than two years later at the Tsar's hunting lodge from typhoid.

The Imperial family in mourning for the Tsar's grandmother, Queen Louise of Denmark, but with a new baby: Grand Duchess Marie. Olga and Tatiana are also in the picture.

1896. Princess Irina, only daughter of Grand Duke Alexander Mikhailovich and Grand Duchess Xenia, standing tall.

1898. Prince Andrew Romanov with his first cousin Grand Duchess Olga in the grounds of the Dowager Empress' Palace. At this time the families of Tsar Nicholas II and his eldest sister Xenia were extremely close, but after the birth of her second son the relationship between the sisters-in-law (the Empress and Xenia) became much cooler. Andrew was to die as late as 1981, having many memories of his Imperial cousins.

1901. The daughters of Nicholas II, Tatiana, Marie and Olga in the year of the death of their great-grandmother, Queen Victoria.

Nicholas II photographed in 1895 with his brother Grand Duke George on the right, and his cousin Prince Nicholas of Greece in the centre. Shortly before Tsar Alexander III's death he telegraphed for a meeting with his sick son, George. Grand Duchess Olga remembered – "believe it or not my father spent whole hours watching by his bedside at night". This was truly a very intimate and caring portrait of a father and son, both very ill. Grand Duke George was to die less than five years later on the 28th June 1899 after years of poor health.

Nicholas II, Empress Alexandra, Grand Duchesses Olga and Xenia and Grand Dukes Alexander and Michael. Photographed in 1900 when they were all in mourning for Grand Duke George. His death, although expected, caused much sadness in the Imperial family. The Dowager Empress was extremely keen for Michael to become the next heir to the throne, as providence had given Nicholas daughters but as yet no son. This was to alienate the young Empress further from her mother-in-law.

Grand Duchess Olga (1882-1960) married Prince Peter of Oldenburg (1868-1924) in the year 1901 at the age of 19. She herself claims she was tricked into it, but some of her letters prove that she was quite happy about the marriage and it was only on meeting Colonel Nicholas Koulikovsky, and after a lifetime of a devoted second marriage to him, that the Grand Duchess changed the history of her first marriage.

Grand Duchess Olga. Her shrewd observations of life at Tsarskoe Selo make her memoirs compulsive reading, although regarding her first marriage she did like to paint herself whiter than white at times.

Grand Duchess Xenia (1875–1960), the Tsar's sister. Here in the Crimea 1897 with her husband, Grand Duke Alexander, and their two eldest children, Prince Andrew and Princess Irina.

By 1899 Xenia had one daughter Irina and two sons: Andrew and Feodor. The birth of these children was to be the cause of the gradual eroding of the relationship between herself and the young Empress Alexandra. Also, Xenia preferred to spend much of her time at Ai Todor, her Crimean estate, away from the capital with her young family.

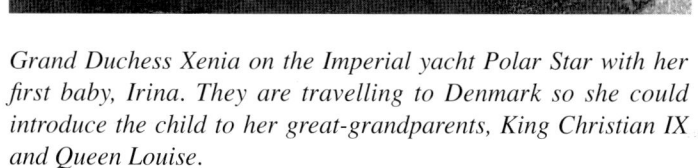

Grand Duchess Xenia on the Imperial yacht Polar Star with her first baby, Irina. They are travelling to Denmark so she could introduce the child to her great-grandparents, King Christian IX and Queen Louise.

After the birth of her seventh child, Vassili, Xenia rarely saw Nicholas, Alexandra or for that matter her husband, who had started to stray even though he considered her a great woman and a great mother.

Grand Duke Michael (1878-1918) in 1902. It was claimed by Poliakoff in "Mother Dear", that the Dowager Empress brought up her son "like a girl, in complete ignorance of men and things of the world".

Empress Alexandra and the boy she so desperately wanted, the Tsarevitch Alexei.

The heir to the throne, the Tsarevitch Alexei in 1906. His birth and chronic ill health were to have a colossal influence on the last years of Imperial power.

Elizabeth Kurakin remembered "a pretty, healthy boy on a blue satin cover, edged with lace, lying on the Empress' chaise longue. As I bent to kiss him the Empress stood behind me, radiantly beautiful in the overriding happiness of a young mother". Little did she realise that haemophilia was to strike less than six weeks after the birth of her beloved son

Grand Duke Nikolai Nikolaievitch (1831–1891). At the time of this portrait his relationship with his wife had broken down and he had fallen in love with a ballerina, by whom he had a second family.

Grand Duke Mikhail Nikolaievitch (1832–1909) – the youngest brother of Alexander II, and the father of Grand Duke Alexander Mikhailovitch, who married Grand Duchess Xenia.

Grand Duke Paul Alexandrovitch (1860–1919). The Romanovs enjoyed fancy dress balls enormously. Here the Grand Duke is photographed at Grand Duke Vladimir's lavish ball of 1883.

Grand Duke George Mikhailovitch (1863–1919), a grandson of Tsar Nicholas I. He married a Greek Princess, who became the Grand Duchess Marie Georgievna (1876–1940). Marie left Russia shortly before the First World War and came to England with her daughters. Many thought the circumstances of her arrival was a trial separation from the Grand Duke who loved her deeply although her feelings for him were cooler. After the revolution he managed to get to Finland and then kept requesting permission to join his wife and family in England. This was refused and the Grand Duke was shot early in 1919. Their daughter Princess Xenia became Mrs Leeds. She involved herself with the woman claiming to be Anastasia and rashly promised she would arrange an interview with the Dowager Empress. In this she broke the Romanov family code.

Nicholas and Alexandra surrounded by their children in the year 1906. From left to right: Anastasia, Alexei, Marie, Tatiana and Olga. They were one of the most photographed families in the world.

The four sisters: Olga (1895-1918), Tatiana (1897-1918), Marie (1899-1918) and Anastasia (1901-1918?).

By 1905 the Dowager Empress said to a lady-in-waiting of the young Empress Alexandra: "She has splendid ideas but she never tells me what she does or expects to do. When we two are together, she always converses about everything but herself. I shall be glad if only she would drop her reserve". Astonished, the lady-in-waiting replied: "Pardon me Madam, but these are the very words the Empress used. She regrets no less speaking with you only on indifferent topics and would be happy if you would let her help you with the work". Such was the lack of understanding between the two Empresses.

The saviour of Russia, Prince George of Greece (1869-1957), who saved the future Nicholas II's life during the 1890 visit to Japan. In an open carriage the pair went through the narrow streets of Ostu, when a Japanese fanatic brandishing a sword attacked the Tsarevitch. Prince George came to his aid with his own walking stick.

The youngest children of Tsar Alexander III were Michael and Olga, who are photographed here a year after their father's death. They had great fun together as children and were extremely close. After both had married unsuitably they fell out, and although they tried to make it up for their mother's sake, their relationship was never to be the same again.

The Tsar with the two sisters, his wife Alexandra and his aunt by marriage, Ella.

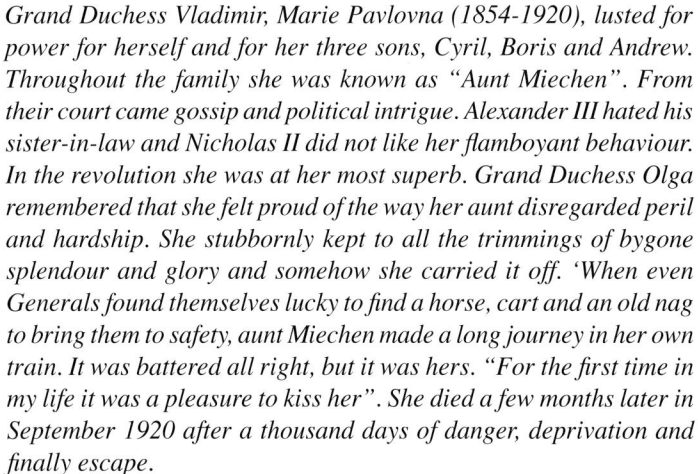

Grand Duchess Vladimir, Marie Pavlovna (1854-1920), lusted for power for herself and for her three sons, Cyril, Boris and Andrew. Throughout the family she was known as "Aunt Miechen". From their court came gossip and political intrigue. Alexander III hated his sister-in-law and Nicholas II did not like her flamboyant behaviour. In the revolution she was at her most superb. Grand Duchess Olga remembered that she felt proud of the way her aunt disregarded peril and hardship. She stubbornly kept to all the trimmings of bygone splendour and glory and somehow she carried it off. 'When even Generals found themselves lucky to find a horse, cart and an old nag to bring them to safety, aunt Miechen made a long journey in her own train. It was battered all right, but it was hers. "For the first time in my life it was a pleasure to kiss her". She died a few months later in September 1920 after a thousand days of danger, deprivation and finally escape.

Grand Duke Cyril (1876–1938). Cyril trampled on other people's feelings and at the coronation of Nicholas II he fell in love with Princess Victoria Melita, who at the time happened to be married to the young Empress Alexandra's brother, the Grand Duke of Hesse. Their love affair and subsequent marriage set Europe's Royal courts ablaze with gossip.

Victoria Melita (1876–1936) was a granddaughter of Tsar Alexander II and also of Queen Victoria. She was determined to marry Grand Duke Cyril and the death of Queen Victoria removed the opposition and allowed her divorce from another first cousin, the Grand Duke of Hesse and by Rhine, to take place. It still took four more years before she and the Grand Duke married. They married without the permission of the Tsar, Cyril was stripped of military rank and although Victoria Melita's lineage was royal she was still not recognised as a Grand Duchess and their marriage was illegal under Romanov family law.

Their banishment ended in 1909 and Cyril and his family could return to Russia. His rank was restored and she became a Grand Duchess. Above, they are photographed with their eldest child, Princess Marie, 1908.

Vladimir who was born in August 1917 became the Head of the house of Romanov after his father, Grand Duke Cyril, in 1938. Cyril had proclaimed himself Tsar and Autocrat of Russia in 1924 during the lifetime of the Dowager Empress. She was opposed to his claim and spoke out against it. Vladimir died in 1992.

Grand Duchess Victoria Melita. Her most notorious action was during the 1917 revolution. On the day before the revolution started she encouraged her husband to break his oath to the Tsar and pledge allegiance to the Duma. They also raised a red flag over their palace. They were the only members of the Imperial Family to do so.

The Grand Duchess Elisabeth following the death of her husband, Grand Duke Serge, in 1905 had, along with the Tsar, become the guardian and chief mentor to Grand Duke Dimitri and his sister Grand Duchess Marie. Although Marie was very young it was decided that she should make a political marriage to Prince Wilhelm of Sweden. She was headstrong and accepted the Prince in order to gain liberty from her aunt. There were, however, too many temperamental and educational differences between the couple and within a very short period of time severe marital difficulties arose. Here photographed around the time of their marriage, Prince Wilhelm on the right, Grand Duchess Marie on the left, and aunt Ella in the centre. Taken in 1908. The birth of their son, Prince Len-nart, in 1909 was not to give the Grand Duchess the joy she so needed or the family life that she so craved. She had never felt at home in Sweden and her husband gave her little affection, on top of which she had no idea how to handle a child. Although she was shown great compassion by the King and Queen of Sweden, she was so full of worries and self-reproach that her life in Sweden was falling into tatters. The only escape route was the annulment of the marriage. In 1913 the Tercentenary of the house of Romanov, she went home to Russia to celebrate and there asked the Tsar's permission to end her marriage. Quite surprisingly Grand Duchess Elisabeth supported her case and took her side.

Grand Duchess Marie, Princess of Sweden, dressed in a folk-costume from the province of Södermanland, of which her husband was Duke. After the divorce she married the Russian Prince Serge Putiatin, a short marriage, and had to struggle in order to support herself as one of the Romanov survivors. She wrote two books of memoirs, and died in 1958.

Prince Wilhelm of Sweden (1884-1965), Duke of Södermanland. He became a successful writer of travel essays, poetry and reminiscences. He never remarried, but lived with Mme Jeanne de Tramcourt as his constant companion for decades.

Prince Lennart, Duke of Småland, was born in 1909 and grew up not knowing his mother, who left the family when he was very small. His father being away a lot, it was his grandmother, Queen Victoria of Sweden, who took charge of the young prince's upbringing. In 1932 Prince Lennart ceased to be a member of the Royal family when making an unequal marriage. Having inherited the small island of Mainau in the Bodensee from his grandmother, he set out to turn this jungle and worn-down palace into the world famous flower park that it is today. Prince Lennart, who was later created Count Bernadotte af Wisborg, also established himself as a skilful and artistic photographer and ecologist. He died in December 2004 at the age of 95.

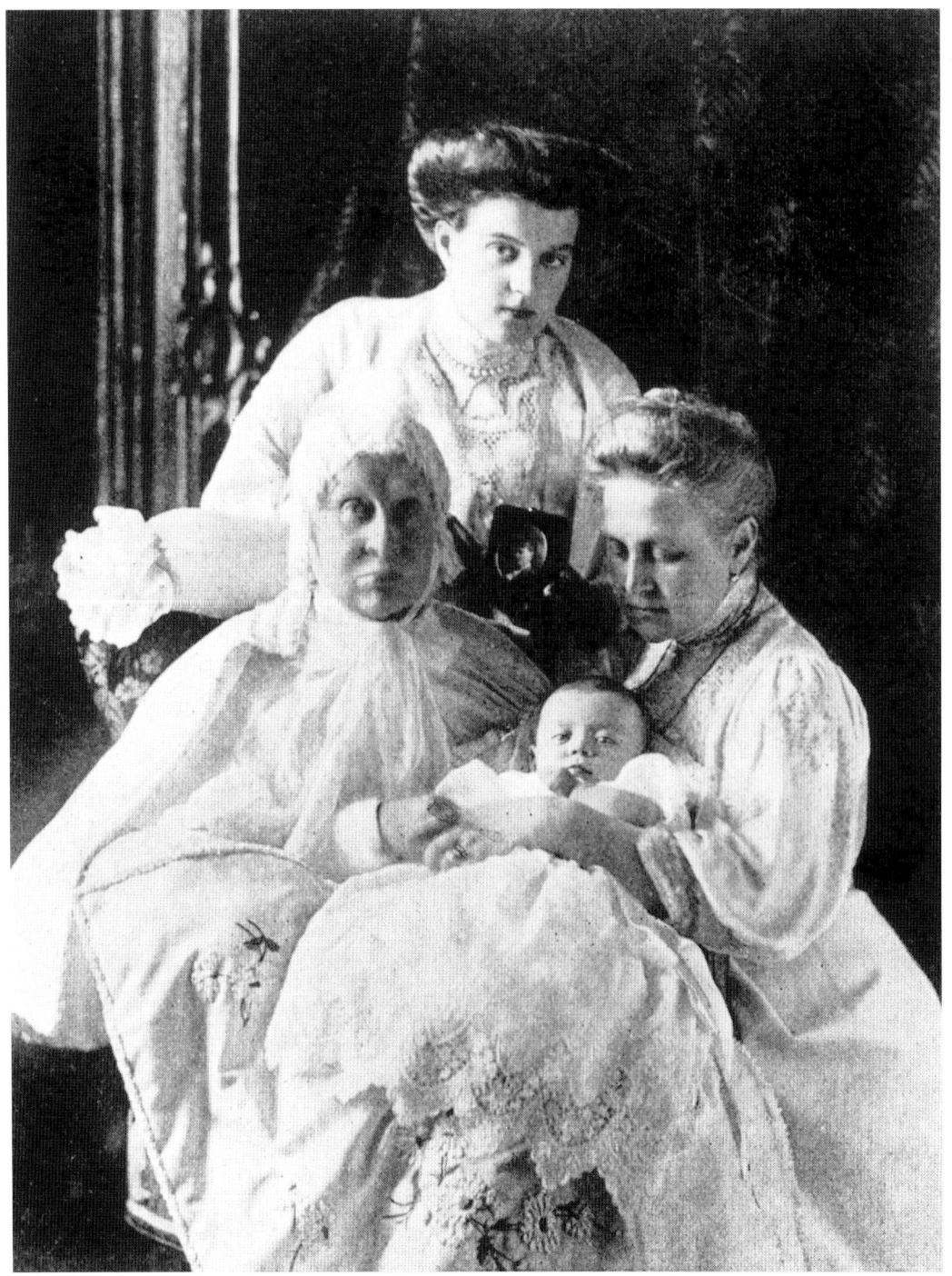

A unique family group, showing five generations of royalty: Grand Duchess Alexandra Josephovna (1830-1911), her daughter Queen Olga of Greece (1851-1926), a miniature portrait of her daughter, Princess Alexandra of Greece (1870-1891), standing: her daughter, Grand Duchess Maria Pavlovna (1890-1958). The baby is her infant son, Prince Lennart of Sweden (1909-2004).

Princess Maria was quite popular during the few years that she lived in Sweden, and an abundance of postcards of her were issued, many of them showing her in various types of hats. In the 1920s, when she was living in Paris, she tried to turn her interest in fashion into a career. She died in Constance, Germany in 1958, having re-established contact with her only surviving son.

Grand Duke Dimitri (1891-1942) in 1914. Another Grand Duke commented: "Dimitri, looked as if he had been made by Faberge". He became a national hero, because he competed in the Olympics and was a favourite of the Tsar and Empress, who treated him like a second son. It was hoped by them, that in time he would marry their eldest daughter, Olga. Unfortunately he started to lead a dissipated life and had a strong friendship with Prince Felix Youssoupoff, which caused many courtiers to speculate that they may have been having an affair. To this day it has never been confirmed that the two most handsome men in Russia were really in love; however, their private notes to each other tend to prove this. Whatever the reason, Empress Alexandra put a stop to the marriage proposal. After Dimitri was involved in Rasputin's murder, Grand Duchess Olga, Nicholas II's daughter, noted: "all hope is lost".

With the murder of Rasputin in December 1916 the Empress Alexandra, here photographed with Grand Duke Dimitri in 1910, sadly realised that her nearest and dearest relatives were involved in treachery against her husband and the Crown. And this was the boy they had treated as a second son and hoped as a husband for one of their daughters.

Osborne August 4th 1909. From left to right: Prince Edward, the future Queen Mary, Queen Alexandra, Princess Mary, The Tsar, Princess Victoria, The Tsarevitch, King Edward VII, Grand Duchess Olga, Grand Duchess Anastasia, Empress Alexandra, Grand Duchess Tatiana, the future King George V and Grand Duchess Marie. This famous photograph was taken when the two families met at Barton Manor on the Isle of Wight. The children played on the beach, and Queen Alexandra was already hoping that her beloved grandson David (Prince Edward) would be interested in one of the elder daughters of the Tsar.

Taken at the same time as the previous picture, the two Royal cousins, Tsar Nicholas II and the future King George V, look strikingly similar in this double portrait.

A unique portrait of a family in mourning. The Dowager Empress Marie and her sister Alexandra Queen of England with the future King George V and Queen Mary in Copenhagen. Believed to have been taken in the year 1906 but unusually Queen Mary appears not to be in mourning for her husband's maternal grandfather, King Christian IX.

Three portraits of the Tsar's children, Marie on the left, in the middle Anastasia and Alexei, on the right Grand Duchess Olga. A member of the family remembered "we often went to the Winter Palace to play with the little Grand Duchesses...then we were happiest, for there we sensed ourselves in a real family atmosphere, simple and calm". The Emperor and his wife held for each other and their children a deep and unswerving devotion and their conjugal happiness was beautiful to see.

Tsarevitch Alexis (1904-1918?) in uniform. Right: The four daughters who called themselves OTMA when they sent joint presents (1914). All had a crush on Grand Duke Dimitri, but with the callousness of Rasputin's murder only Olga, the eldest, mentioned him in diaries or letters afterwards. Standing: Marie, Anastasia and Olga. Seated: Tatiana.

A grand alliance, 1914. Two great grandchildren of Queen Victoria, Grand Duchess Olga and Prince Carol of Romania (1893-1953), who it was hoped would be united in matrimony. Carol's mother, Queen Marie of Romania was in two minds about the prospect of her son being united to the great Romanov dynasty, because she feared Olga would bring haemophilia into the Romanian Royal House.

On the Standart. The Dowager Empress with her hand on the Tsar's knee. A wonderfully intimate shot of the Tsar, his mother and her pet. This photograph was taken in the summer of 1912 on the Empress' name day.

Right: The Imperial Yacht, Standart, took the family to Constanta Romania for their last state visit abroad. It seems neither set of parents would push their children into a loveless marriage and left it to the hands of fate. Grand Duchess Olga seemed very uninterested in her second cousin and he seemed far more interested in her younger sister Marie who was barely fifteen years old. So Olga happily passed up the chance to become the future Queen of Romania.

State visit to Constanza, Romania 1914. Princess Ileana remembered her mother, the future Queen Marie, in a flurry about the arrangements as a Tsar had never visited Romania before! In old age she also recalled that for her this was a photograph of ghosts. Seated, from left to right: Grand Duchess Marie, Empress Alexandra, Grand Duchess Tatiana, Crown Princess Marie of Romania (1875-1938), Grand Duchess Olga holding Prince Mircea of Romania (1913-1916). Standing: King Carol of Romania (1839-1914), Grand Duchess Anastasia, Princess Marie of Romania (1900-1961), Prince Carol of Romania, Princess Ileana of Romania (1909-1991), Crown Prince Ferdinand (1865-1927) of Romania, Queen Elisabeth of Romania (1843-1916) and Tsar Nicholas II. Seated on the floor: Tsarevitch Alexei and Prince Nicholas of Romania (1903-1978). Queen Marie wrote: "I for one was sad when the hour for parting came and our guests again took possession of their floating abode, which was once and for all to carry them out of our lives".

1911 Grand Duke Michael and his Natasha (1880-1952). Their love affair, her divorce and then marriage to him caused an international scandal, because after the Tsarevitch Alexei he was the heir apparent to the Imperial throne.

Natasha. Maurice Paleologeue, the French Ambassador to Russia, remembered her with delight. He saw a slender young woman of about thirty and said her whole style revealed great personal charm and refined taste. Her chinchilla coat opened at the neck gave a glimpse of a dress of silver grey taffeta with trimmings of lace. Her pure aristocratic face is charmingly modelled and she has light velvety eyes. Around her neck a string of superb pearls sparkled in the light. There was a dignified sinuous soft gracefulness about her every movement. After the revolution Natasha was to escape to the west. During World War II she was to sink further and further into poverty. In 1952 she lay dying of cancer in a charity ward. Such was the end of the woman who was married to the last Tsar of Russia.

1912. Georgi, Count Brassow, the only son of Grand Duke Michael. After his father's murder in 1918 there were justified fears for the boy's safety from the Bolshevik danger. He escaped with his nanny, posing as an Austrian refugee. His mother and half sister Tata escaped by a different route. Georgi was then looked after by the Danish Royal House. After 1920 the Dowager Empress received Michael's son a few times and even saw his mother, Natasha, twice. She left him a substantial legacy. In the 1920's he was given the title Prince George Romanovsky Brassow. He could not inherit the vacant Russian crown as he had been born out of wedlock. In July 1931 his sports car skidded off the road and hit a tree. Georgi's friend was killed outright and he himself died two days later.

The Imperial daughters, Olga and Tatiana, come of age. Less than 18 months between them, the sisters are photographed in June 1914 when the younger daughter Tatiana had just reached the age of 17. They were given a sumptuous ball by their grandmother, the Dowager Empress, and came home at four in the morning with their father who, like many a father, had waited for them to finish enjoying their first grown-up occasion.

On board the Standart, away from the petty intrigues of court, the Tsar and his Empress enjoy the last summer of peace in June 1914.

Grand Duchess Olga with her mother, Empress Alexandra, and her mother's lady-in-waiting, Elizabeth Narishkin-Kurakin, who also left a memoir: "Under Three Tsars". These reminiscenses were slanted against the Imperial family and get more and more spiteful in the last years of the regime. This was the woman that the Empress considered a friend.

On the following pages are a number of unique photographs, developed from a collection of old, mostly damaged, glassplates. The quality of these pictures is not always the best, but since these rediscovered images do give a new and very informal view of the Imperial family, they deserve to be published. Left, the Tsar's two eldest daughters, Olga and Tatiana in 1913 with their lady-in-waiting in the palace courtyard at Livadia. Here the whole family relaxed, according to Anna Virubova. The whole palace, including the rooms of state, were lightly and beautifully furnished in white wood and flowered chintzes, giving the effect of a hospitable summer home, rather than a palace.

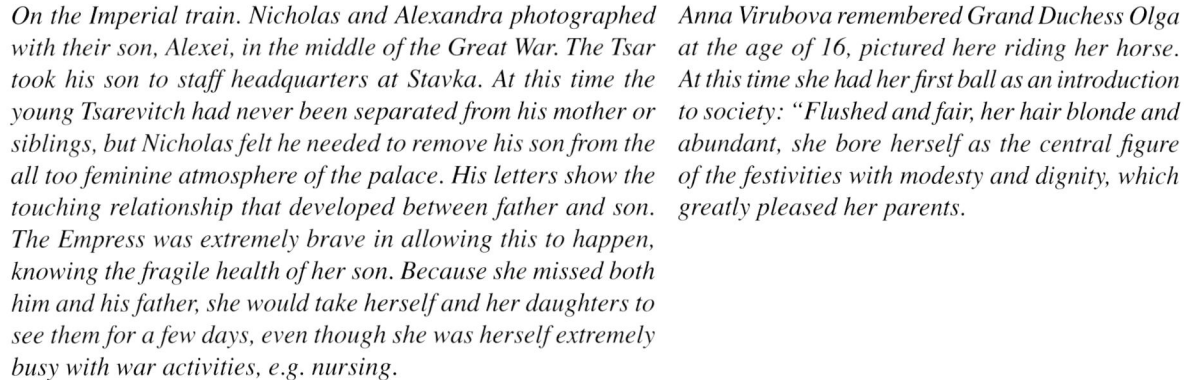

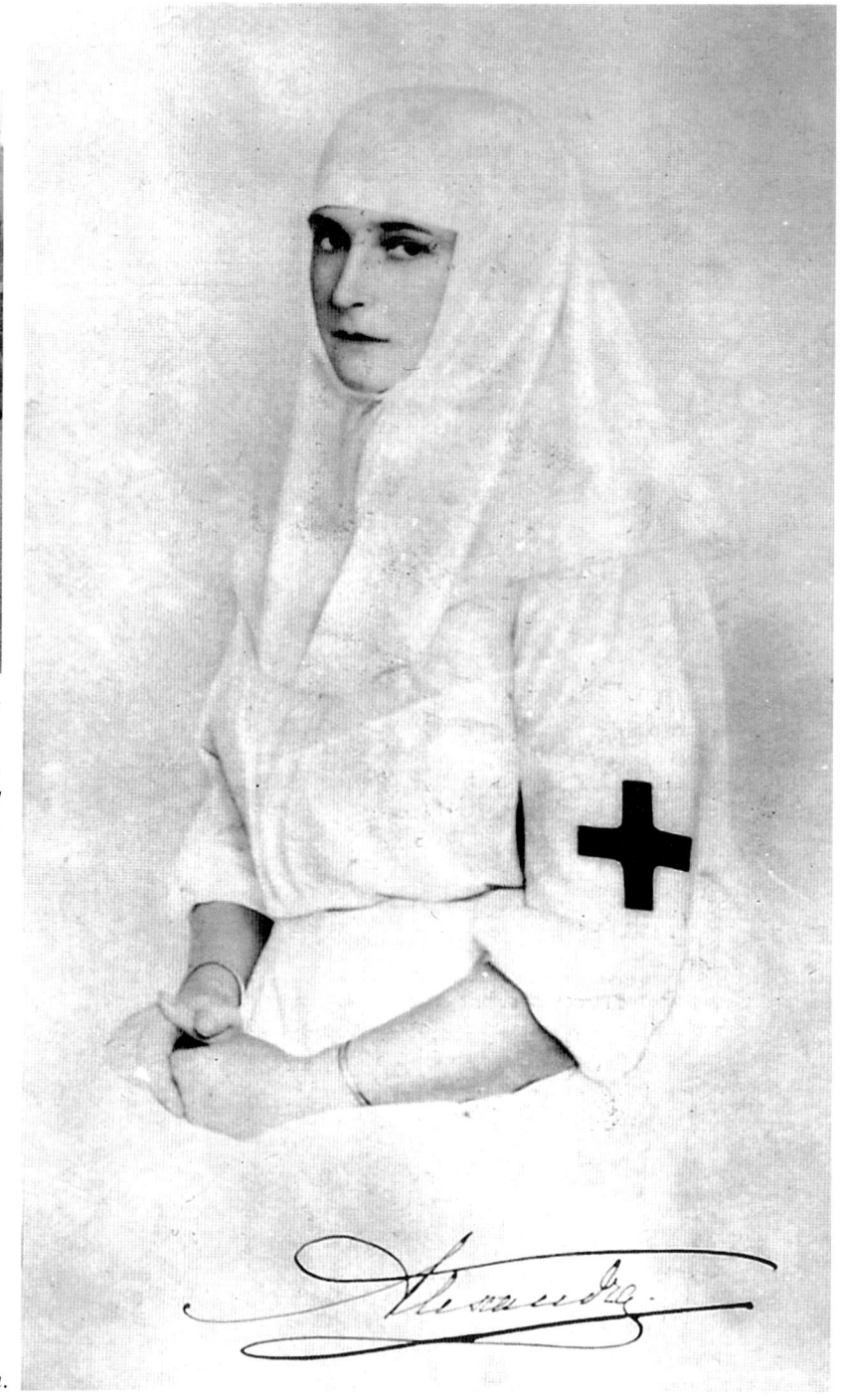

On the Imperial train. Nicholas and Alexandra photographed with their son, Alexei, in the middle of the Great War. The Tsar took his son to staff headquarters at Stavka. At this time the young Tsarevitch had never been separated from his mother or siblings, but Nicholas felt he needed to remove his son from the all too feminine atmosphere of the palace. His letters show the touching relationship that developed between father and son. The Empress was extremely brave in allowing this to happen, knowing the fragile health of her son. Because she missed both him and his father, she would take herself and her daughters to see them for a few days, even though she was herself extremely busy with war activities, e.g. nursing.

Anna Virubova remembered Grand Duchess Olga at the age of 16, pictured here riding her horse. At this time she had her first ball as an introduction to society: "Flushed and fair, her hair blonde and abundant, she bore herself as the central figure of the festivities with modesty and dignity, which greatly pleased her parents.

Empress Alexandra in nurse's uniform.

70

A bouquet of Imperial summer pictures...

Above left: Grand Duchess Marie at the age of nearly 15. Already a beauty, she had a naturally sweet disposition, which her younger sister Anastasia took particular advantage of.

Above right: The Tsar, smoking, with gun in hand. Queen Marie of Romania remembered her cousin Nicky: "He was charming as ever and I found myself continually watching him again and again. It struck me how very lovable he was with his low voice and gentle eyes";

Right: A tennis party with the Tsar and his younger daughters, Anastasia and Marie, and officers of the Standart.

Left: The Tsarevitch sweeps the deck. Both his parents continually explained to him the necessity of avoiding falls or blows, but he was an active child who came near to death several times because of childish mishaps.

Extreme left: Empress Alexandra brought her children up simply, despite their station in life. Their manners were unassuming and natural without a single trace of hauteur.

Grand Duke Alexander and Grand Duchess Xenia with their offspring in the year 1909. Left to right: Prince Nikita (1900-1974), Princess Irina (1895-1970), Princes Andrew (1897-1981), Dimitri (1901-1980), baby Vassili (1907-1989), Feodor (1898-1968) and Rostislav (1902-1968). The Dowager Empress insisted, that these grandchildren were also grand dukes and grand duchesses of Russia and not merely princes and princesses.

Grand Duke Alexander and Grand Duchess Xenia and their entire family consisting of six sons and a daughter. Irina is standing with her mother, her eldest brother Andrew is seated to the right, Feodor, Rostislav, Nikita, Vassili and Dimitri are all in the same portrait. The Grand Duchess had practically retired from public life due to ill health and disenchantment with her husband. The family rarely appeared on public occasions, although Prince Andrew did go on several tours with Nicholas II's family and had a close relationship with his uncle. This photograph was taken in 1916.

1914. Grand Duchess Xenia Alexandrovna (1875-1960), the elder of the two sisters of the last Tsar.

1914. Grand Duke Alexander Mikhailovitch (1866-1933). His memoirs in several volumes were very successful and were published in many different languages.

1914: Princess Irina of Russia (1895–1970) and her fiancé, Prince Felix Youssoupoff (1887–1967). He was one of the handsomest men in Russia. He was also the heir to one of the richest estates and, as if he needed any more prestige, he married into the Imperial House. The wedding of Irina, to Prince Felix Youssoupoff took place on the 9th February 1914 and it was in fact, the Tsar who gave her away, as was traditional in Imperial marriages.

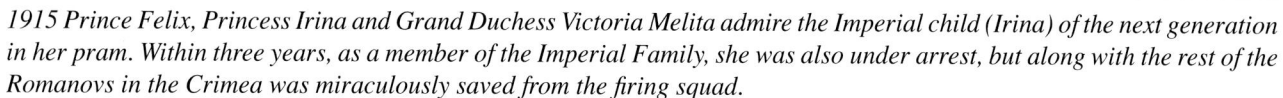

1915 Prince Felix, Princess Irina and Grand Duchess Victoria Melita admire the Imperial child (Irina) of the next generation in her pram. Within three years, as a member of the Imperial Family, she was also under arrest, but along with the rest of the Romanovs in the Crimea was miraculously saved from the firing squad.

Top right: Grand Duchess Xenia with her first grandchild, who was born on the 8th March 1915. Xenia became a grandmother at the early age of 39. By 1916 she was unwell and from the autumn went to Ai-Todor as the situation in Petrograd deteriorated.

1915. The Dowager Empress becomes a great grandmother in the last days of the Empire. Here she is photographed with her great grandchild, Princess Irina Youssoupoff.

Left: Tsar Nicholas II with his daughter Tatiana, her brother Alexei and their cousin Nikita (Xenia's son). In 1916, the second year of the Great War, the Tsar's regime started to weaken dramatically. The Tsar remarked to Sir J Hanbury-Williams, that "he had been doing a bit more of the publicity and photography business for the war effort".

Right: Grand Duke Michael became Tsar for a day in the mayhem of the 1917 revolution. He carried on living at Gatchina and in February 1918 he was arrested and sent to Perm. In June 1918, he and his faithful secretary and friend Johnson, were taken by force to a forest where they were shot.

The last formal photograph, taken in December 1916, of Tsar Nicholas and his children surrounded by the Cossacks. From left to right: Anastasia, Olga, The Tsar, the Tsarevitch, Tatiana and Marie. Within three months the privileged house of Romanov was to be shattered forever.

Grand Duchess Marie, the Tsar's third daughter. Of all the children of the Tsar, her simplicity and charm of manner meant that the men who were guarding the family, found her the easiest to talk to.

The Tsars eldest daughters photographed on the balcony of the Governor's house. Baroness Buxhoeveden said at this time: "Olga (on the right) took on much of the worries for her parents safety and the family's well-being. This turned the bright young girl of 22 into a prematurely middle-aged woman". This photograph somewhat denies this description of her.

Above right: Another photograph of the Imperial children taken in the summer of 1917, which included the Tsarevitch. The tranquil lake which they all often sat by in the palace grounds is pictured above. This was to be a time of relative peace for the family, before imprisonment turned harsh with the prospect of going to Siberia, where Tsars had once sent political prisoners. Ironically the children of the Tsar were not under arrest, but it was a joint decision that they decided to remain with their parents, even though they had been advised to stay with their grandmother, the Dowager Empress, and go to Livadia so that they could remain safe. By the end of 1917 the children had become political prisoners as well.

The daughters of the Tsar imprisoned. They were as superlatively groomed as English ponies with their perfect skin and lovely faces. They deserved a far better fate.

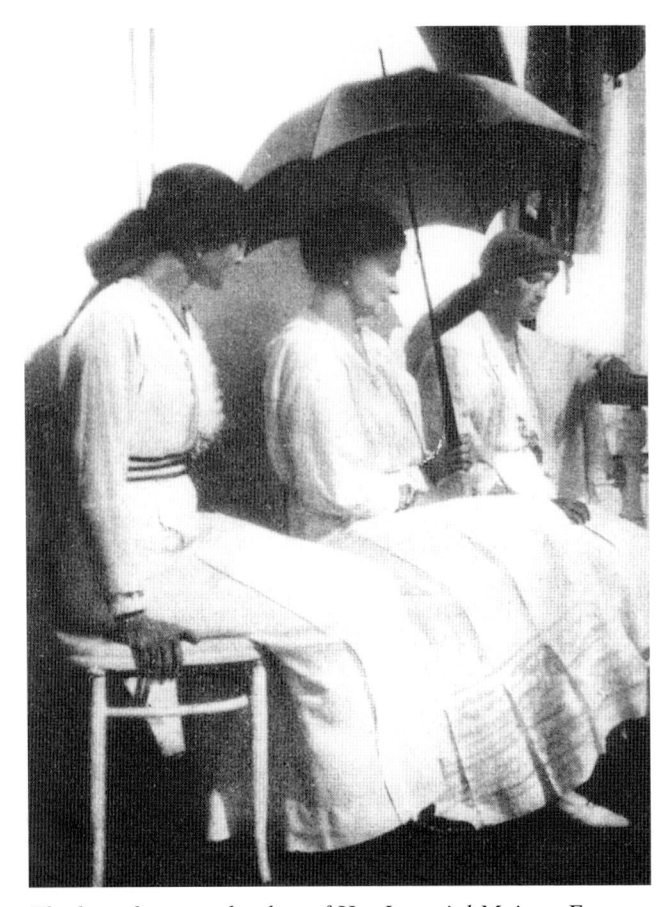

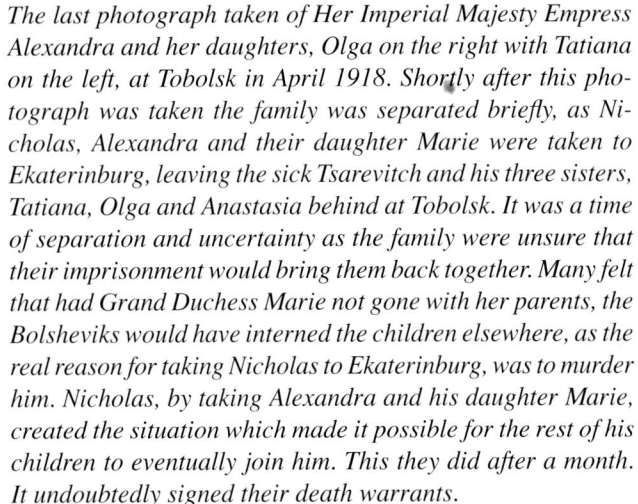

The last photograph taken of Her Imperial Majesty Empress Alexandra and her daughters, Olga on the right with Tatiana on the left, at Tobolsk in April 1918. Shortly after this photograph was taken the family was separated briefly, as Nicholas, Alexandra and their daughter Marie were taken to Ekaterinburg, leaving the sick Tsarevitch and his three sisters, Tatiana, Olga and Anastasia behind at Tobolsk. It was a time of separation and uncertainty as the family were unsure that their imprisonment would bring them back together. Many felt that had Grand Duchess Marie not gone with her parents, the Bolsheviks would have interned the children elsewhere, as the real reason for taking Nicholas to Ekaterinburg, was to murder him. Nicholas, by taking Alexandra and his daughter Marie, created the situation which made it possible for the rest of his children to eventually join him. This they did after a month. It undoubtedly signed their death warrants.

The House of Special Purpose. In May 1918 the dethroned Tsar was ordered to leave Tobolsk for Ekaterinburg. He left with his wife, the Empress, and his third daughter, Grand Duchess Marie. Nicholas' other children, Olga, Tatiana, Anastasia and the Tsarevitch were left behind at Tobolsk as the boy was ill. They were to join their parents a few weeks later. This photograph was taken in May 1918, shortly before the second stockade was built. Now they were truly prisoners. The windows were whitewashed and they could not see out and they were not allowed to go to church. There was no privacy. The bathroom and lavatory were shared with the guards and less than two months later they were put to death in the vaulted semi-basement. The cellar became a museum until 1945. During the autumn of 1977 the Ipatiev House was demolished.

The survivor of Ekaterinburg: Joy, the Tsarevitch's beloved pet Cocker Spaniel. For some reason that has never been explained, the dog was found running around aimlessly in the courtyard several days after the family's murder by the Bolsheviks. The dog, which was blind, was taken to England where, after several years, it died at Windsor.

The Dowager Empress leaves Russia in April 1919 on HMS Marlborough. She had refused for some months to go, feeling that she should remain in Russia with her family. Finally Queen Alexandra sent an urgent letter to her sister. This did the trick and the Dowager Empress agreed to leave on the 4th April 1919. She declared she would leave only if allowed to take along the colony of loyal people who still surrounded her. This Captain Johnson agreed to.

A perplexed Queen Alexandra (1844-1925) leaves Marlborough House to go to the station to greet her sister, the Dowager Empress. The latter had, thanks to her, miraculously escaped the Bolsheviks. Alexandra was so distressed, that some of her entourage tried to discourage her from going, but she insisted, and along with the rest of the Royal Family, apart from the Prince of Wales, they were all there at the station, that being Royal etiquette.

Grand Duchess Xenia on board HMS Marlborough. Four generations of the Romanov family left Russia on this ship: the Dowager Empress, her daughter Xenia, her granddaughter, Princess Irina, and her great-granddaughter, the little Princess Irina and her father, Prince Felix Youssoupoff. Also on board were five of Grand Duchess Xenia's sons, the Princes Feodor, Nikita, Dimitri, Rostislav and Vassili. Xenia's three eldest sons did not approve of Felix, feeling that Rasputin had been a good man. They were appalled that Felix had tarnished the good name of the Imperial family. Their relationship with Irina remained the same and all through the years of exile she was always welcome. Not so with Felix, with whom they were all to have a colder relationship, even Prince Feodor, who actually lived with Irina and Felix in the early 1920's.

Prince Felix Youssoupoff and his wife Princess Irina leave Russia on HMS Marlborough. The Princess had been extremely brave during the revolution, a true granddaughter of Alexander III, she had returned to the Winter Palace to see Kerensky to outline to him the appalling treatment of her grandmother the Dowager Empress, who was under arrest. Although many members of the Romanov family were also under arrest none could believe that the Princess, who was usually so shy, would stand up to Kerenskij. As she left the Winter Palace, which Kerenskij had taken over as his headquarters, old servants of her grandfather who were still there went down on their knees and kissed the hem of her dress.

Princess Irina (1915-1983), a great-granddaughter of the Dowager Empress and the only child of Felix and Irina, was the youngest person of the main Romanov line to escape the revolution aboard this ship.

Irina, and her husband, Prince Felix Youssoupoff.

Princess Irina. Not much is written about Irina, apart from the court cases that her husband involved her in, and that she was a fragile beauty. She was, however, made of sterner stuff, and the saving grace for her was a film by MGM, called Rasputin and the Empress. It had portrayed her as a rape victim of Rasputin. As she had never met Rasputin, the Prince and Princess Felix sued the film company, a case which they won, and were awarded damages to the tune of 100.000 dollars. You could say that Hollywood gave her back her splendour to a very handsome degree. Irfe was the fashion house created by Prince Felix Youssoupoff and his wife Irina: she was to become its most famous model as she was considered a great beauty. Even the Youssoupoffs, who had left Russia far richer than any other members of the family, (they had brought along two Rembrandts), were still short of money. In 1923 they had gone to New York to sell a number of their jewels. When they left on HMS Marlborough they had managed to take some very valuable pieces with them, but by the autumn of 1923 life was becoming increasingly difficult. Unfortunately when they arrived in the US, customs seized the jewels. Eventually customs released the jewels, but Prince Felix had to deposit 80% of their value, which caused him to sell the Rembrandts. This was another long saga, which brought the pair unpopularity and made them notorious in the USA. Cartier also came to their aid, but this was a dreadful situation for Irina as she was in the somewhat embarrassing position of going to a function in the evening in jewels that once belonged to Catherine the Great, and having to wash her clothes in the bath when she came home. If it wasn't so ludicrous it would have been funny.

The Landwehr Canal 1920 and inserted "Miss unknown". The woman who was claiming to be the Grand Duchess Anastasia had thrown herself into the canal. Saved by a policeman she had been taken to the Elisabeth Hospital for mental patients. She then managed to create such a stir that the whole of Berlin was talking as if this was Tsar Nicholas II's daughter. The issue was to divide the surviving members of the Romanov family. Only the Dowager Empress, who refused to receive her, remained above it. For over sixty years "Anna Anderson" was to keep the world intrigued as to whether she was indeed a lost princess. The DNA tests eventually proved she was not.

The real Grand Duchess Anastasia (1901-1918?), photographed in June 1917 in the early days of her imprisonment. The youngest daughter of Tsar Nicholas II had turned sixteen in January of that year and her wit and darts of humour kept many amused at this difficult time.

Right: The Dowager Empress makes her last public appearance in the winter of 1925, supported by her Cossack Yachik, who adored the Empress and wrote his memoirs about his time with her. She was attending a thanksgiving at the Russian church. It had been handed over to the parish in Copenhagen after the Soviets had laid claim to it.

Left: Queen Alexandra, the Queen Mother, and her sister the Dowager Empress. The Dowager Empress had come to stay with the Queen for the wedding in April 1923 of the Duke of York and Lady Elizabeth Bowes-Lyon. On the day of the wedding, when they were all waiting to go out on the balcony, the Dowager Empress had been advised that perhaps it should just be the main family. This she gladly accepted. At the moment the balcony doors were opened she took Queen Alexandra's arm and said "shall we go out dear", leaving the rest of the family horrified. After this incident King George V made sure that any public appearances the Dowager Empress made with him, Queen Mary and Queen Alexandra, they would all walk in line together.

The Villa Hvidore, photographed in the year of the death of the Dowager Empress. After her death it was sold and the proceeds were split between her heirs, the Grand Duchesses Olga and Xenia. Grand Duke Michael's son, Georgi Brassow, was paid privately by the Grand Duchesses before the sale.

The formal 80th birthday portrait of the Dowager Empress in November 1927. By this time she was known to the Danish people as "the lady of tears", but she was a stronger character than that and refused to accept in her mind the death of her sons and grandchildren. She was also extremely clever in never allowing the Romanovs to accept the claimant Grand Duke Cyril to proclaim himself Autocrat of all the Russias and refused to receive him or his wife, Victoria Melita. After her death the family was split in their decision to accept the claim.

This private image of the smiling Dowager Empress in her 81st year at Hvidore, her last home. Here they claimed the old Empress played solitaire with her memories. She also had a king's ransom in jewels hidden under her bed. After her death there were many problems trying to sell the jewels in the market of the day. Queen Mary bought many items, which are still worn by the present Queen and the ladies of her family. In the memoirs of Grand Duchess Olga, Queen Mary was criticised for obtaining the jewels at less than their value. It has recently been proved that she did, however, pay the correct price for the jewels she acquired from the Russian cousins.

Grand Duchess Xenia in the garden of Frogmore Cottage, the house that King George V kindly gave her as a grace and favour residence. Xenia adored living in England and she loved her cottage, which was actually quite large. Apparently, when her servants first saw King George V, they went down on their knees, thinking it was the Tsar. The two cousins resembled each other enormously.

The grand wedding on the 31ˢᵗ May 1923 was the marriage between Prince Feodor and Princess Paley (1903-1990) who was the daughter of the second marriage of Grand Duke Paul. This was considered a very advantageous marriage (sadly it did not last). The Dowager Empress could not attend as she had been taken ill in London after the wedding of the Duke of York to Lady Elizabeth Bowes-Lyon and stayed on with her sister for the rest of the summer. The guests at the Paris wedding in 1923 are pictured here, left to right: Grand Duke Dimitri with Grand Duchess Xenia in front, Prince Feodor with Princess Irina Pavlovna Paley, Grand Duke Alexander behind her, Princess Olga Paley and Grand Duchess Marie Pavlovna and the page boy.

1925. Grand Duchesses Olga, with her sister Xenia at extreme right and Xenia's son, Prince Andrew, centre, and daughter Irina to the left. Throughout the years of exile the Tsars sisters were to have a difficult and strained relationship. This was because Grand Duchess Xenia kept her position by remaining within the British Court and also because she looked down on Olga for marrying a commoner, albeit from an aristocratic background. On top of this, Olga had not divorced her first husband but had merely had the marriage annulled by the Tsar. Grand Duchess Xenia, who had quietly separated from her own husband, thought that her sister had somehow let the family down.

Prince Irina with her mother, Grand Duchess Xenia, in the Lattice Garden at Hampton Court. The Princess would spend long periods in England as her mother grew older, where she was away from Prince Felix. As the Princess put it: "his thirst for life always gadding about". She found she had to get off the merry-go-round, as it exhausted her. In April 1960 Grand Duchess Xenia died quietly at Wilderness House, a grace and favour residence belonging to the Queen. She had outlived her brothers by over 40 years, and since her arrival in England there had been three Kings and now a Queen on the throne. With the death of her beloved cousin King George V, Grand Duchess Xenia had moved further away from the British Royal Family. King Edward VIII suggested that she move from Frogmore Cottage to Wilderness House at Hampton Court. The Grand Duchess did not like it, as it was too near the river and made her asthmatic, but felt she was unable to complain. During the war years she spent sometime living on the Balmoral Estate but saw little of King George VI and his family. Until Queen Mary's death she did at least have a link with the crown, but from 1953 onwards she seldom saw the major members of the Royal Family. She did give one writer an interview in old age, only because Princess Mary had requested it. There are rumours that she wrote her autobiography, really just a private memoir, but so far it has never surfaced. With her death and that of her sister a few months later, the two people with the authority to talk about their brother, the Tsar, were gone. Luckily for history, Grand Duchess Olga gave her memoirs to Ian Vorres, which he wrote in an appealing way.

Left: Prince Felix Youssoupoff, pictured in old age. Right: Prince Felix and Princess Irina in 1962. Despite Prince Felix being notoriously homosexual, they were married for 53 years and were quite devoted to each other. Irina forgave her husband his indiscretions and, as a member of the family put it, she simply adored him. In Paris they were welcome in the grand houses, the Duke and Duchess of Windsor's amongst them, where Irina could enjoy the trappings of her once gilded youth. Prince Felix by this time wore much cosmetics to appear younger, but instead the rouge and the eye make-up made this once handsome prince into a pantomime dame. In spite of this, before his death, Irina had become more watchful of him. As she grew more frail, she became somewhat reclusive. She had a heart attack three years after his death and died in March 1970 aged 75. Together they rest at St Genevieve Des Bois.

Grand Duchess Olga, photographed in 1921 with her second husband, Colonel Koulikovsky (1881-1956), and her two sons, Tihon and Guri. They had had a less dramatic escape from the country that Olga loved. Although Colonel Koulikovsky came from a good family, he was still a commoner which was protection for Olga, but only slightly. On their journey through the countryside they managed to meet General Koutepov of the White Army, who recognised the Grand Duchess and gave them his own coach which was coupled to a train leaving for Rostov. Surprisingly, in the countryside through which she travelled, peasants crammed onto the banks to stare at the former Imperial Highness who was shabbily dressed with a baby in her arms. It was not without menace, as at one point on the journey someone tried to unloose the couplings of the train. Her young, brave husband managed to climb across the roofs to the driver, otherwise the story could have ended in tragedy. Some six weeks after this the Grand Duchess gave birth to her second son, Guri. They had a hazardous journey to Novorossiysk where the streets were full of starving refugees, who were running away from the terror and typhus which gripped the city. Olga and her husband with their two small sons ran for shelter at the Danish consulate, where she had her biggest stroke of luck. She met Flag Captain James, who knew her and had danced with her many years before. He took her aboard HMS Cardiff for tea. They then managed to get a tiny merchant ship, which took them to safety. They first went to Prinkipo, then to Constantinople and then to Belgrade, where His Majesty King Alexander met her with due reverence. From there she left for Denmark, arriving around Easter 1920.

Princess Marina, the Duchess of Kent, visiting her Romanov cousins in Cooksville, Canada, in the 1950s. From left to right: Ruth and Guri Koulikovsky, Agnete and Tihon Koulikovsky, Princess Marina, Grand Duchess Olga and Nikolaj Koulikovsky. [Picture from the book; Tihon – The Tsar's Nephew by Hans Neerbek]

Above left: Tihon (1917-1993) and Guri (1919-1984) Koulikovsky as young soldiers, saluting their parents, Nikolaj Koulikovsky and Grand Duchess Olga. [Picture from the book; Tihon – The Tsar's Nephew by Hans Neerbek]

November 1960. She was the last member of the dynasty, who was born in the purple, and the very last Russian Grand Duchess, the daughter of Tsar Alexander III. Grand Duchess Olga died in Canada in a small apartment over a shop. This is truly a story of riches to rags, but somehow Olga had remained happy to the end. Her lack of pretension, her kindness and obvious intelligence made her a serene individual. Her marriage to Colonel Koulikovsky had been one of such extreme happiness, a case of "love at first sight". At the end of her life she also commented: "However little I had to give, I don't think I withheld anything to serve my dear country as a Romanov".

The famous picture, taken nearly 90 years ago in Tobolsk, of the Imperial family enjoying some sunshine on the roof: Olga, Anastacia, Nicholas, Alexi and Tatiana. Standing: Marie.

Death of a dynasty. The entire Russian Imperial Family was murdered brutally on the night of July 16th 1918. The girls are presumed to have died in agony because of the jewels sewn into their corsets offering a degree of protection. Neither Alexei nor Anastasia have ever been found. Some people feel that Lenin was against killing children and both brother and sister were below the age of 18. Princess Alice, Countess of Athlone went to see the premier of the film "Nicholas and Alexandra". When she left the cinema, the manager asked her if she enjoyed it. She replied: "Horrid, horrid, horrid. Nicky and Alicky were never like that, and I do not believe that they died so dreadfully" and with that she flounced out of the cinema!

William Mead Lalor
ROYALTY BEFORE THE WARS
2003, 96 pages, 180 ill. large format
ISBN 91-973978-5-7

This collection covers "The Golden Age of Royalty", the period between the turn of the century and up to the first World War. Splendid formal portraits along with large family groups, and with the emphasis on the minor Royal and Princely families of Europe. **SEK 280:-**

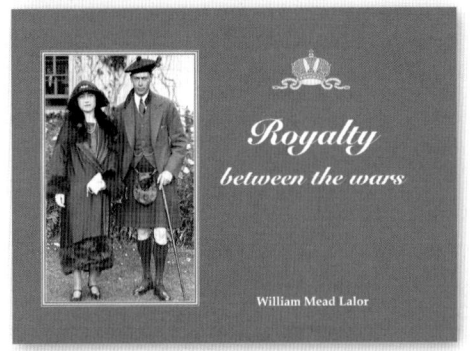

William Mead Lalor
ROYALTY BETWEEN THE WARS
2005, 96 pages, 136 ill. large format
ISBN 91-630-8284-5

Volume two in this series deals mostly with the 20s and 30s. The majority of Royal Families had seized to reign and in many cases gone into exile. A truly unique collection of a hard-to-find pictorial documentation. **SEK 280:-**

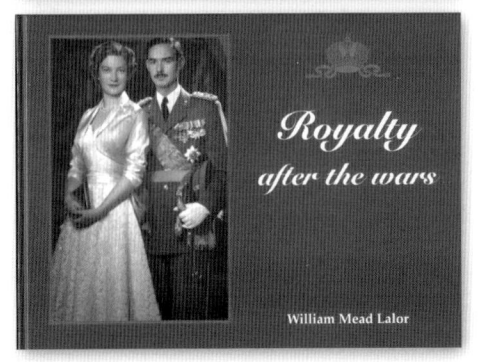

William Mead Lalor
ROYALTY AFTER THE WARS
2001, 96 pages, 159 ill. large format
ISBN 91-973978-2-2

The third volume in this series deals with the period from the end of World War II up until around 1970. A difficult period for the collector of Royal pictures, but the author has a truly unique collection, from which it was possible to put together this most enjoyable album. **SEK 280:-**

HM KING MICHAEL I OF ROMANIA
[SM Le Roi Michel Ier de Romanie]
A Tribute - Un Hommage
[in English and French] ISBN 91-973978-3-0
2001, 96 pages, 113 b/w and 25 colour ill.

King Michael - his life in pictures, with text by his daughter and son-in-law. A unique life, a unique book! Dedications by the King of Spain and by the Prince of Wales. Pictures from the private albums of the Romanian Royal Family. **SEK 360:-**

Marlene A. Eilers
QUEEN VICTORIA'S DESCENDANTS
1997 2nd edition 192p 168 ill. ISBN 91-630 5964-9

This is an encyclopedia of European Royalty. Queen Victoria and her Albert had 9 children and 42 grandchildren. Today there are close to 1000 descendants, residing all over the world. Many of them are Kings and Queens, Princes and Princesses, Dukes and Barons. They belong to various Royal families, e.g. Spain, Sweden, Denmark, Norway, Russia, Prussia and Hesse, but there are also ordinary people, workers, actors and secretaries. Apart from a very detailed genealogical section, this volume has a wealth of interesting facts and stories about the descendants. It is richly illustrated, the majority of the pictures having been contributed by the descendants themselves. **SEK 295:-**

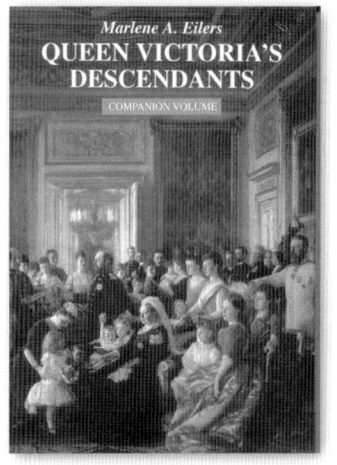

Marlene A Eilers
QUEEN VICTORIA'S DESCENDANTS COMPANION VOLUME
2004 84 pages 83 illustrations [in English]
ISBN 91-973978-8-1

Here is the long awaited companion volume to Queen Victoria´s Descendants. An expert in the field, the author has spared no effort when trying to correct and up-date the genealogy as well as the text and picture sections. The result is a highly informative and readable volume, to be enjoyed as a complement to the original book. **SEK 195:-**

Samuel C Dotson
Genealogie des Fürstlichen Hauses LIECHTENSTEIN seit Hartmann II. (1544-1585)
ISBN 91-973978-4-9
2003, 232p, 62 ill. [in German]

A complete and detailed genealogy of the Princely House von und zu Liechtenstein, the largest Princely family, reigning over the smallest Principality in Europe. **SEK 325:-**

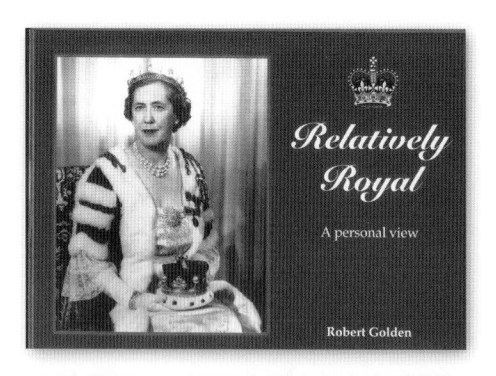

Robert Golden
RELATIVELY ROYAL
A personal view
2000, 96 pages, 140 ill. large format.
ISBN 91-973978-1-4   **SEK 280:-**

Two glorious photo albums, covering the extended family of Queen Victoria, including the Battenbergs, the Fifes, the Cambridges, the Connaughts, the Harewoods, the Athlones and many others. Entertaining text by an author who actually knew many of these Royals and semi-Royals personally.

Robert Golden
THE GOLDEN BOOK OF ROYALTY
- Relatively speaking
2002, 96 pages, 160 ill. large format.
ISBN 91-973978-5-7   **SEK 280:-**

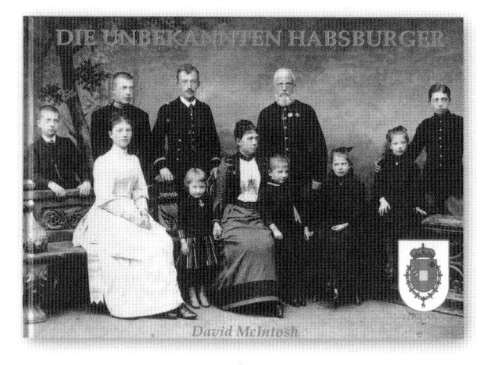

David McIntosh
DIE UNBEKANNTEN HABSBURGER
THE UNKNOWN HABSBURGS
2000, 96 pages, 120 ill.
[in English and German]
A unique collection of pictures and pedigrees of the Tuscany (Toscana) branch of the Habsburg dynasty. Leopold Wölfling, the Crown Princess of Saxony and Johann Orth - they are all there. Pedigrees included.   **SEK 280:-**

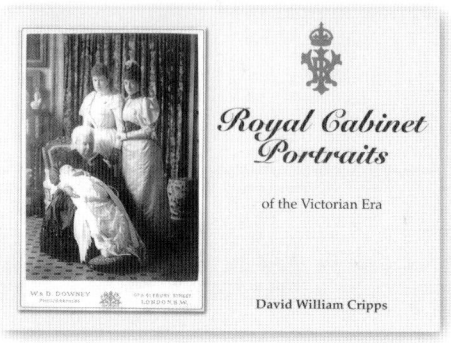

David William Cripps
ROYAL CABINET PORTRAITS
of the Victorian Era
2003, 96 pages, 190 ill. large format
ISBN 91-973978-6-5
A new Royal Picture Album, focusing Queen Victoria's children, grandchildren, great grandchildren and other close relatives. Many unique portraits from the Courts of Russia, Prussia, Hesse and from other Royal families.   **SEK 280:-**

Hans Neerbek
TIHON
The Tsar's Nephew
2005 c. 240 pages richly illustrated [in English]

Not all the Romanovs perished in the Russian Revolution. Among the survivors were the Tsar's mother, the Dowager Empress, and two sisters, Xenia and Olga. The latter made it to Denmark with her husband, Nikolaj Kulikovski and their infant sons, Tihon and Guri. The boys grew up in Denmark, and Tihon was known to his friends as "Kuli". This biography is written by one of his Danish friends, and it is a picture of a man, intimately connected to World History and to the tragic Romanov dynasty.   **SEK 240:-**

Antoinette Ramsay Herthelius
Ted Rosvall
ASTRID
1905 – 1935
2005, 80 pages, 106 ill. large format
ISBN 91-975671-0-8
A memorial album focusing the legendary Queen Astrid of the Belgians, Princess of Sweden. Published in connection with the centenary of her birth, this unique album includes pictures from her childhood, youth, marriage and short time as Crown Princess and Queen. Text in Swedish and English.   **SEK 260:-**

In preparation

David McIntosh
DIE GROSSHERZÖGE VON
THE GRAND DUKES OF
OLDENBURG
2005, c96 pages, 100 ill.
[in English and German]

The history and genealogy of a German Dynasty. A unique collection of pictures and pedigrees are included in this readable monography.   **SEK 280:-**